China Rare Animals and Ecological Protection Series

I0145908

Tales of the Père David's Deer

Compiled by Ding Yuhua

1 Plus Books

China Pictorial Press

Tales of the Père David's Deer

©2017 China Pictorial Press

©2017 1 Plus Books   English Edition

ISBN-13: 978-0-9994263-8-8

Publishing manager: Yu Jiutao

Managing Editor: Fang Yunzhong

English Translator: Zhong Yuanshan

Special Editor: Sophia Liu

Book Design: Ai Qing

Published by 1 Plus Publishing & Consulting in the USA

www.1plusbooks.com

San Francisco, USA

Preface

China faces a heavy task in promoting economic growth as a developing country. Nevertheless, with regard to global climate change and environmental protection, the Chinese government, in recent years, has been advancing a development concept of "innovation, coordination, green, open and sharing", taking green development and a low-carbon and circular economy to the next level. Unprecedented priority has been given to eco-environmental protection. Wild animals are the spirits of nature, and those endangered rare species are very sensitive factors in the eco-environment. With special habits and unique survival wisdom, they harmonize perfectly with the successive beauty of the different seasons and, along with China's diverse geographical environment and rich fauna and flora, constitute the natural environment without which we cannot exist.

China has a long history of thousands of years. It not only

has a profound cultural heritage, but also rich ecological diversity, and a wide variety of wild animals is one of the highlights. China has always been committed to the ecological/environmental cause and has made great progress in the wild animal protection. According to the 2011 National Wildlife Resource Survey, China's rare and endangered wildlife protection has achieved remarkable results: the survival status of a number of endangered wild animals such as the Golden Monkeys, Asian elephants, Père David's deer, giant pandas, crested ibis, Tibetan antelopes, etc., has improved and significant population increases. Among the 420 species listed in the *Lists of Widelife under Special State Protection*, the populations of 341, are no longer considered endangered. At the same time, however, the situation of wildlife protection in China is still very serious, 87.7% of the wild animals are face a squeeze on their living space due to habitat reduction, fragmentation, deterioration, human activity, etc.; many important habitats and bird cluster activity areas and migration channels are challenged by land development, agricultural reclamation, environmental pollution and other threats.

It is of great significance to protect wild animals, save rare and endangered wild animals and maintain biodiversity and ecological balance according to law, for promoting the harmonious development of humans and nature and enhancing the construction of a true ecological civilization. I hope that this colorful, dynamic life pictorial on Chinese wild animals will enable the general adult readers to embark on a unique trip through the natural beauty on Earth, while drawing their attention to the fate of China's rare wild animals and encouraging them to become actively involved in the protection movement along with us. We can build a new pattern of broad participation in wildlife protection and make due contributions to the construction of a beautiful China with a good ecological civilization and improvement of the global environment!

The Compiler
Nov.2017

CONTENTS

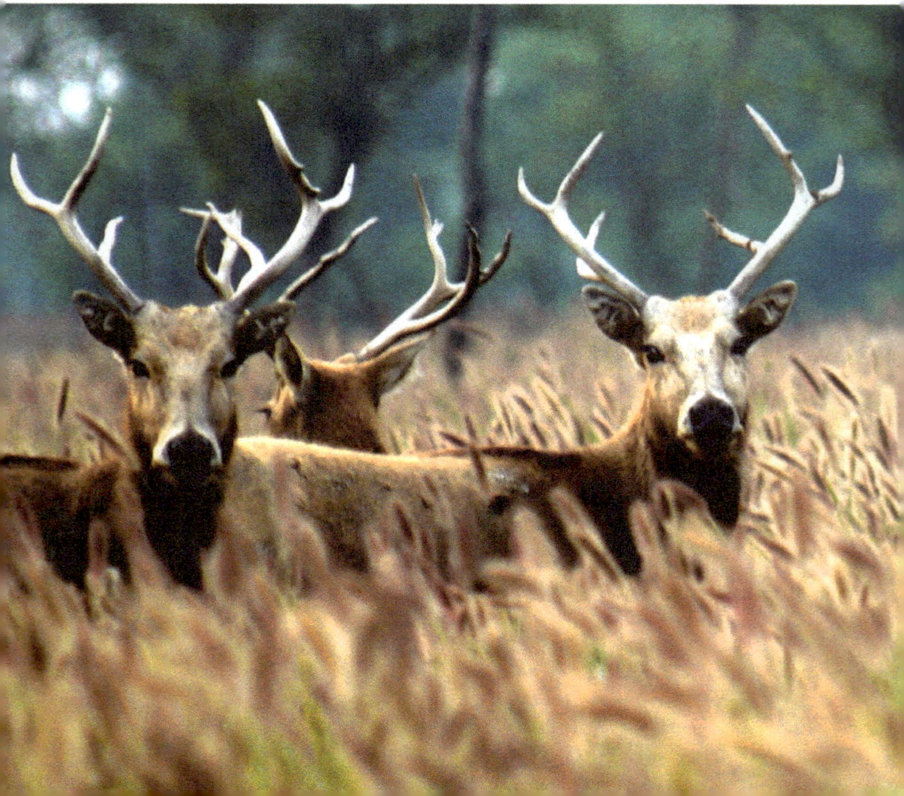

I

'The Four Unlikes'
Native to China

The Père David's deer is a relatively large member of the deer family. A male one can have a head-and-body length of up to 2 meters, anda height of one meter, and a weight of about 200 kg. Its antlers are long and the long tines of the branched antlers point backward. A dropped antler can stand still when placed upside down. A female deer is relatively small in size and weighs about 140 kg. It has no antlers, and is docile, timid, gregarious and good at running. Its pregnancy lasts for nine months and a half. The Père David's deer has the antlers of a deer, the face of a horse, the hooves of a cow and the tail of a donkey, hence the name of "Four Unlikes".

There are five subspecies in the history of the Père David's deer, that is, the double-branch species, Lantian species, Jinnan species, Taiwan species and davidianus species. Only the latter continues to exist.

It's not a horse though it has a face like horse.

It's not a deer though it has deer-like antlers

It's not a cow though it has cow-like hooves.

It's not a donkeys though it has donkey-like tail.

• Special shapes of the Père David's deer.

• Père David's deer in swamps.

Distribution of Père David's deer in China

The Père David's deer was native and unique to China in ancient times, when there was a wide coverage across at least half of national territory. Based on fossil distribution, its ancient coverage range extended to Xiangfen of Shanxi in the west, to the seaside islands in the east, to Kangping of Liaoning in the north, and to Hainan Island in the south. The activity areas of Père David's deer were very wide. Among the aforementioned regions of unearthed fossils, the largest number was excavated in Taizhou, Nantong and Yancheng in Jiangsu Province.

Since 1956, China has been reintroducing Père David's deer, ending a history of the species being native to the country but extinct. It has flourished with steadily increasing numbers. From the 1950s to 1970s, the species was mainly housed in the zoos of Beijing, Harbin and Guangzhou. After the 1980s, the emphasis switched to creating new habitats in Beijing Nanhaizi Milu Park, Dafeng Milu Nature Reserve in Jiangsu and Shishou Milu Nature Reserve in Hubei.

• Jiangsu Dafeng National Père David's Deer Nature Reserve.

• Hubei Shishou National Père David's Deer Nature Reserve.

• Beijing Nanhaizi Père David's Deer Garden.

Tales of the Père David's Deer

Finally, in 2010, Jiangsu Dafeng Milu Nature Reserve was able to reintroduce the species to the South Yellow Sea Beach Wetland, producing the first totally wild deer in China in modern times.

☐ Distribution of the Père David's deer in the world

In 1869, the first pair of living Père David's deer left China for the London Zoo. In the ensuing 30 years, many countries transported living specimens from Beijing Royal Hunting Garden to establish further foreign colonies.

By the end of 1986, living Père David's deer were distributed in 156 breeding sites of 23 countries across six continents. Among these breeding sites, 83 were in Europe, 50 in North America and 14 in Asia.

By 2009, there were a total of 206 breeding sites around the world, and while those in China increased from six in 1986 to 56 in 2009, ensuring it became the country with the most Père Da-

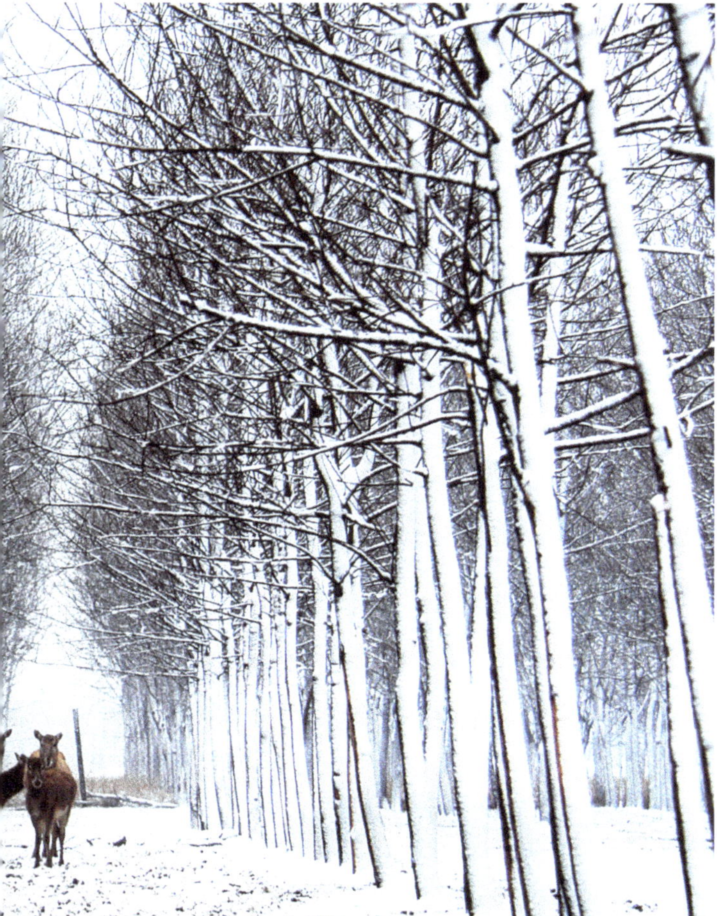

vid's deer.

In recent years, domestic population development has achieved a new breakthrough in China. The Père David's deer has been regaining its former wild behavioral traits, with strong recognition capability and natural protection awareness in the wild, and was able to achieve successful births and raising young in a completely natural environment. The Père David's deer has returned to nature successfully.

☐ Sanctuaries for saving the species

For more than 100 years, Woburn Abbey in the U.K., the U.S. Wildlife Conservation Research Center, and the Beijing Nanhaizi MiluPark, Dafeng Milu Nature Reserve in Jiangsu and Shishou Milu Nature Reserve in Hubei have made great contributions to the development of the Père David's deer population, and have been duly honored as sanctuaries for saving and protecting the species.

In 1895, only 18 Père David's deer remained in the world and were fed in Woburn Abbey, which became the birthplace of the present line.

After the Second World War, the U.S. Wildlife Conservation Research Center introduced the Père David's deer for the first time and gradually developed into a major scientific research base.

In 1985, Beijing Nanhaizi Milu Park for the

• Père David's deer in Woburn Abbey in the UK.

first time reintroduced 20 Père David's deer from Woburn Abbey. At present the number has grown to more than 2,000, enabling the park to reproduce the former royal hunting garden.

In 1986, Jiangsu Dafeng Milu Nature Reserve introduced 39 Père David's deer from London. After decades of continuous development, it has achieved the world's largest population of the Père David's deer, and become the model of saving endangered species and restoring a wild population in the original place.

In 1994, Shishou Milu Nature Reserve in Hubei introduced 40 Père David's deer from Beijing Nanhaizi Milu Park. After years of development, it has now become a pilot in multi-point stocking.

To date, the total number of the five major Père David's deer concentrations accounts for the vast majority of the world's Père David's deer. They play an important role and have a significant impact on the salvation, protection and development of the species.

- Père David's deer in Research Center on Natural Conservation in the Smithsonian Institution.

- Père David's deer in Beijing Nanhaizi Milu Park.

• Père David's deer in Dafeng
 Milu Nature Reserve.

• Père David's deer in Shishou
 Milu Nature Reserve.

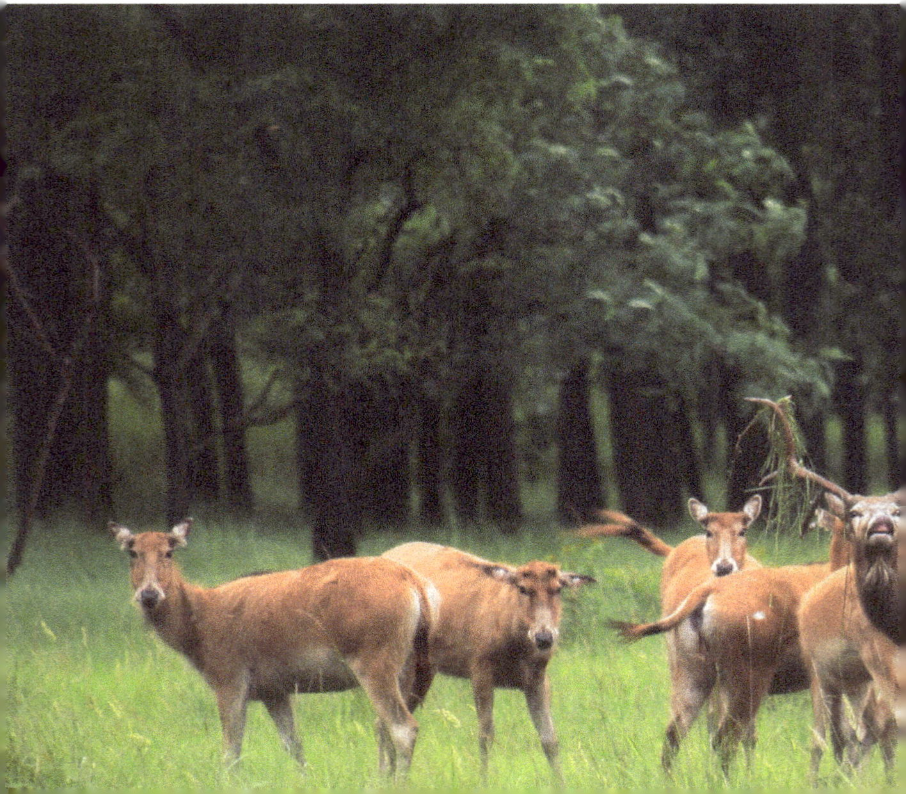

II

History of Père David's Deer

Origins and Disappearance of the Père David's Deer

The Père David's deer originated in the plains and swamp lands of the Yangtze River Valley and the central part of the Yellow River Valley about 3 million years ago. It was concentrated in Yunmengze (present-day Hubei Province) in ancient China, and later gradually extended to the eastern part of China and even the swamplands and wetlands along the coast of the Yellow Sea. More than 1,000 years ago, the Père David's deer often appeared in Yangzhou and Taizhou areas of Jiangsu, only to decline in the early 18th century, when the last wild specimen disappeared in the

• Pursuit in Greenfields.

wilderness near QiaotouTown of Taizhou City, Jiangsu Province.

The Père David's deer lived in China for nearly 3 million years. More than 3,000 years ago, there were about 100 million wild deer, but the 100 years ago, only 18 Père David's deer remained in the world and extinction seem assured. During this period, however, the 11th Duke of Bedford acquired the remaining 18 deer for large sum of money and nurtured the herd at his stately home of Woburn Abbey, not far from London. The current world population stems from those 18 British-based Père David's deer.

• About 2 million years ago.

• 1.2 million years ago.

• 500,000 years ago.

• 10,000 years ago.

Père David's deer leave China

In 1865, French missionary Armand David, found a species of deer in the Nanhaizi Royal Hunting Garden in southern suburbs of Beijing, and he spent 20 silver bars to buy a skull and two pieces of skin of these deer and shipped them to France. In 1866, Alphonse Milne-Edwards, a French biologist, identified and confirmed the remains were a new deer species. In 1867, Armand David announced this conclusion that caused a sensation in Europe. In the following 30 years, many zoos in European countries sought living specimens of the species from the Qing Dynasty government.

• Armand David.

• David looking at the deer.

The United Kingdom took the initiative. In 1867, they captured four adult Père David's deer in the Royal Hunting Garden in Beijing. However, due to lack of experience in their care, the four deer were dead before they could be shipped to England. The skin and skull of one of themwassent to the British Museum, and its bones were shipped to the London Royal Women's College.

In 1868, the British again managed to capture a pair of six-week-old Père David's deer with the help of Ya Ming, the person in charge of the Royal Hunting Garden in Beijing, and sent them to Robert Swinhoe, British envoy in China. In August 1869, the Père David's deer was escorted by a British diplomat to London Zoo. This is the first time that the Père David's deer had been transported alive out of the country.

In 1887, the Berlin Zoo shipped back six Père David's deer taken from the Royal Hunting

Garden in Beijing, of which five were male and one was female.

On April 21, 1888, Japan's Tokyo Zoo got a pair of live Père David's deer from Beijing Royal Hunting Garden.

On July 16, 1895, the 11th Duke of Bedford, the owner of Woburn Abbey, bought a male Père David's deer from an animal businessman to begin his work of saving the species, followed by two females in 1901.In 1901, the Duke of Bedford bought two female Père David's deer from an animal businessman.In the six years from 1895 to 1901, the Duke spent much money to buy 18 Père David's deer, to form the only remaining herd in the world, with contributions from Paris, Berlin, Manchester and Antwerp, and began nurturing the herd at Woburn Abbey .

Re-introduction of the Père David's Deer

The Père David's deer is a rare animal endemic to the Chinese region. However, for various historical reasons, they left their native homeland to achieve survival in foreign countries. From 1956, China began to re-introduce the Père David's deer and rebuild its population.

In the spring of 1956, the British government presented two pairs of Père David's deer to China, which were housed in Beijing Zoo.

At the end of 1973, the Zoological Society of London let two pairs of Père David's deer return home, again to Beijing Zoo.

In 1980, Harbin Zoo exchanged animals with a zoo in the Canada, obtaining a pair of Père David's deer.

By the end of 1982, a total of 10 Père David's deer had returned from overseas, and were kept in the zoos in Beijing, Harbin, Guangzhou, Baoding, and other places.

At the end of 1984, the total number of Père David's deer in China increased to 12, mainly in Beijing Zoo.

In August 1985, Woburn Abbey selected 22 Père David's deer for dispatch to China, of which 20 were nurtured in Beijing Nanhaizi Milu Park (former site of the Royal Hunting Garden), while two were sent to the Xijiao Zoo in Shanghai.

On August 14, 1986, the World Wildlife Fund (WWF) selected 39 Père David's deer from seven zoos and parks in London to give them to China, all being placed in Jiangsu Dafeng Père David's Deer Nature Reserve.

After coming back to China, the deer experienced re-domestication and behavior reshaping in their original homeland and finally achieved normal breeding and expansion. At present, there are three main populations in China, mainly in the Nanhaizi Milu Park in Beijing, Dafeng Milu Nature Reserve in Jiangsu and Shishou Milu Nature Reserve in Hubei.

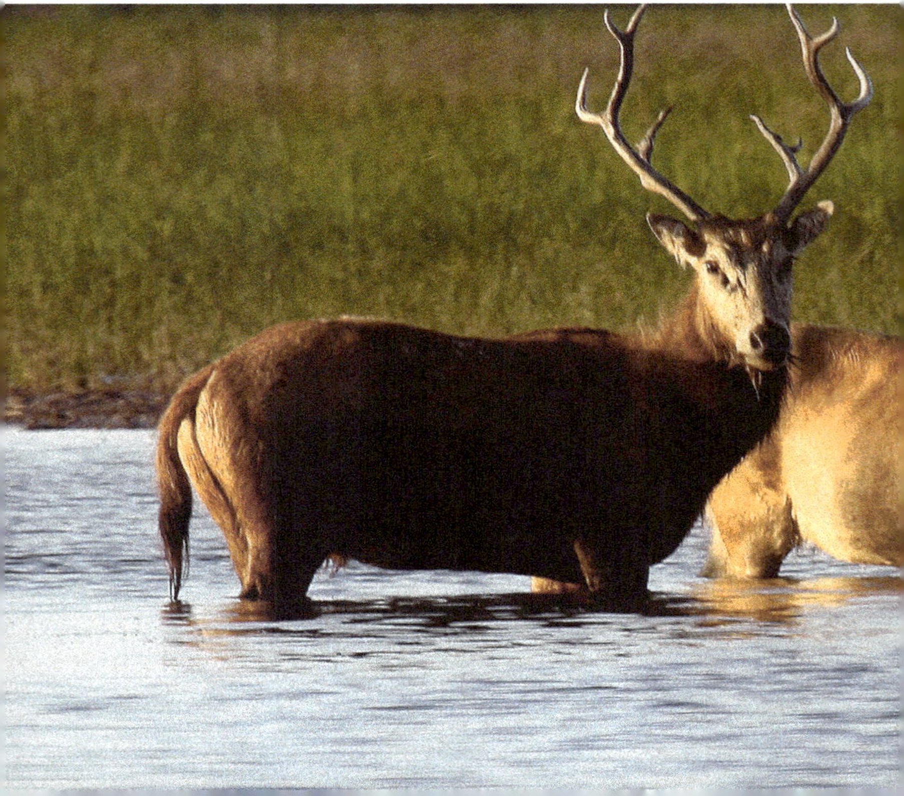

III

Physical Characteristics of Père David's Deer

'The Four Unlikes' Features

The face of a Père David's Deer seems like that of a horse: The face of a Père David's deer is very special. It is not only the longest among all known deer, but looks very much like the face of a horse. The elongated face originated from its eating habits. The Père David's deer is a wetland animal and likes to eat grass, especially aquatic plants. In order to eat plants growing up to 30 to 40 cm under the water, evolution created a suitable long face for the task.

On the upper one-third of the face, the Père David's deer has a pair of big eyes, and there is an orbital gland below each eye corner.

• Horse face.

• Père David's deer face.

The orbital gland is closed under normal circumstances, but opens when danger looms; indeed, in a severe shock, the two orbital glands open.

The antlers of a Père David's deer: Unlike the antlers of other deer species, those of the Père David's deer are branched, the long tines pointing backward, and all the tips of the branches are at the same level, so that, if cut off, they could be reversed and stood upright without toppling. Other deer species also have branches, but the long tines point forward, and all the tips are not at the same level.

People can determine the age of a Père David's deer through its antler. A fresh horn on the head of a Père David's deer is called the "velvet antler".The velvet antler adds a branch every year. At the age of five, the basic shape of the antler branch of the Père David's deer becomes fixed and unchangeable. After the age of six, between one and four small twigs will grow on the outer side of the first branch of the antler, and a few small sarcoids (wart-like growths) appear on other branches. There are many small round sarcoids of a pearl-like size around the outer side of the antler roots,and zoologists call these "pearl plates". On the antler branches are also some grooves of different depth, which serve as natural and beautiful decorations on the antler.

• A fresh velvet antler.

• A two-branch velvet antler.

• A three-branch velvet antler.

• A four-branch velvet antler.

• A five-branch velvet antler.

• A fixed-shape antler.

• A dropping velvet antler.

• A bone antler.

• A Père David's deer uses its tail to drive away insects.

• Some Père David's deer raise their tails.

The tail of a Père David's deer seems like that of a donkey: The tail of a common deer is mostly short, usually only 10 cm long. Only the Père David's deer has a very long tail, which is more than 30 cm long, and occupying almost one-third of body length. A drooping tail can reach the hock like that of a donkey. Such a long tail is the result of living in swampy wetlands. The wetland environment abounds in blood-sucking insects, and a long tail can help the Père David's deer to drive them off. The tail also has the role of maintaining balance. When walking or running, the Père David's deer often use its tail in such a way. When a herd of the Père David's deer run together, the front deer often raise their tails almost like a flag to ensure those following don't stray.

The hooves of a Père David's deer seem like those of a cow: The feet of a Père David's deer, also called hooves, seem like those of a cow. A Père David's deer has four hooves altogether. Usually the first and the fourth hooves are hanging in the air, the second and the third hooves land on the ground, and provide support. Between the second and the third hooves is a layer of aponeurosis, like the webbed feet of

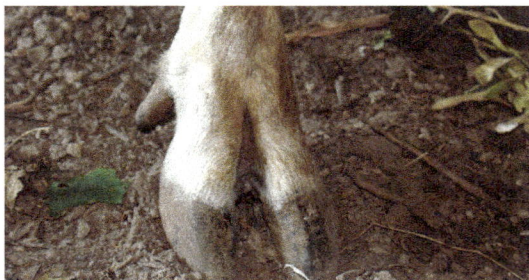

• A hoof of a Père David's deer.

• A hoof of a cow.

ducks. When a Père David's deer stands or walks on muddy land, the second and the third hooves will open and level the aponeurosis between the two feet, increasing the contact area with the ground and preventing their feet from getting stuck in the mud. When swimming, a Père David's deer will also open the aponeurosis between the feet, increasing the contact area of the hooves with water and so enabling the body to float. It can continue to move forward at quite a speed.

A Père David's deer has four stomachs

A Père David's deer has four stomachs, known as a 4-room stomach, from front to back known as the rumen, net stomach, petal stomach and true stomach. A rumen is like a large warehouse. A lot of fodder eaten by a Père David's deer is first stored in it and fermented through its peristalsis. A net stomach has many grids on its wall, like the net. A petal stomach is divided into many layers, and the chewed fodder enters the petal stomach from the net stomach and then gets into the true stomach. The true stomach is the real stomach of the Père David's deer, and grows stomach glands to secrete digestive juice and do digestion.

IV

Breeding Populations of the Père David's Deer

The Père David's deer is a large mammal. Under normal circumstances, a male deer can breed at the age of three when it weighs 150 kg; a female deer can breed at the age of two when weighing 120 kg.

The breeding process of the Père David's deer includes the stages of estrus, mating, pregnancy, calving, and breast feeding.

Every year, June to August form the estrous period. Male and female become estrous at the same time, ensuring smooth mating. The pregnancy last 280 to 290 days.

The lactation period of the Père David's deer is about 90 days. In the later period of lactation, a baby deer will suck milk while learning to eat grass. When the baby deer masters the capability of eating grass, it will be weaned by its mother. After that, the small deer will move around with the herd and find its own food.

• Estrous male Père David's deer.

• Mounting (mating).

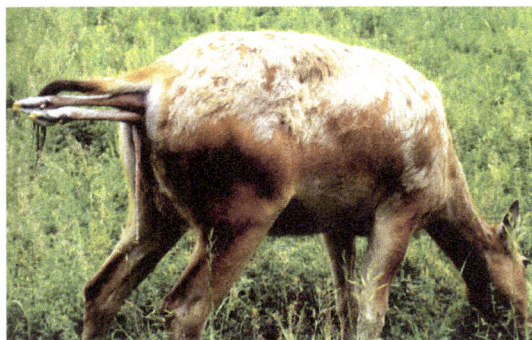

• A Mother Père David's deer giving the birth.

• A newborn baby.

• A one-week old Père David's deer.

• A two-week old Père David's deer.

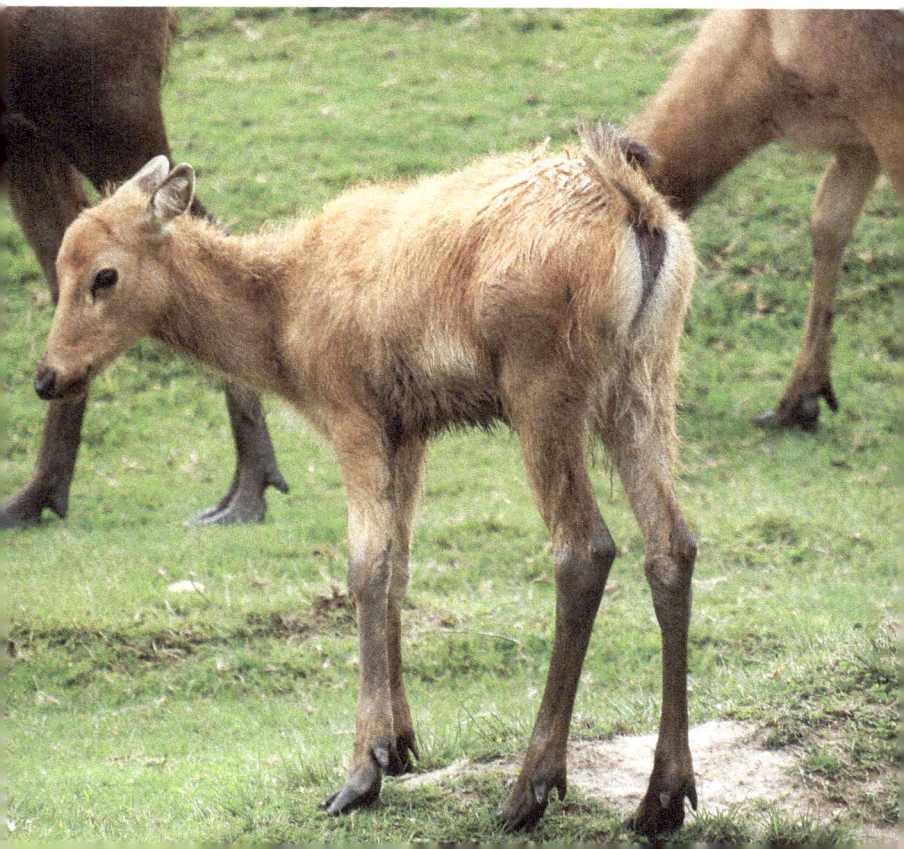

• A two-month old Père David's deer.

V

Group Life of the Père David's Deer

Estrus and Courtship

Spring is the estrous period, the period, female deer emit a special smell and, in the absence of wind, this smell is relatively stable in the air about five meters above the ground and diffusing horizontally in the shrubs and grass. The male deer becomes intoxicated by this mysterious smell. Then, adult males begin to decorate themselves; they paint mud on the back, and use their antlers to pick the grass as a decoration, which is a symbol of might in the eyes of the Père David's deer; the male hopes to win female favor in this way. In the estrus, male deer become irritable; they send out bursts of calls, pick the earth from the ground, rub their faces on trees, and confront or even fight each other.

Behaviors of an estrous male Père David's deer

• Rubbing its face on a tree.

• Painting mud on its back.

• Fighting in the water.

Behavior of male deer in fighting

• Two males fight each other.

• Tussle with all their strength.

• A roaring deer king.

☐ Polygamy in Père David's Deer Groups

In the kingdom of the Père David's deer, there is a strict hierarchical order. In their estrus period, although many male deer hover around the female and glare at them eagerly, they dare not to act rashly. Because among all males, only the king deer has the right to mate. The other males would be driven out ruthlessly or even suffer violent attacks if overstepping the prescribed limits. Therefore, the vast majority of the male deer are likely to spend through their lives without producing offspring.

• A king deer and its"concubines".

• An infant deer less than one-month-old.

Infant Père David's Deer.

From March to May each year is the season of birth for the Père David's deer. An infant deer can stand up on its feet 15 to 20 minutes after its birth, and then go to seek its mother's milk. When the infant deer has finished sucking milk, it will take a rest, lying in covert grass.

The hair of a newborn deer is brown and red, with more than 160 spots on both sides of the body. These spots are white, like plum blossom, and so are often called plum-blossom spots. After some 30 days, these the plum blossom spots will naturally disappear.

• A group of infant deer.

☐ Childhood of Père David's Deer

Père David's deer infants are never alone, as they have a lot of brothers and sisters. On summer morning, after enjoying mother's milk, they lie in the grass to rest; in the afternoon, especially at sunset, they stay together affectionately, or run and play on the grass in a very harmonious way.

• Be affectionate.

• Some running infant deer.

☐ Foster Mother Deer

A female Père David's deer only gives birth to one child a year. During lactation, the mother will only care for her own baby and it is rare to see a mother feeding two babies. In the summer of 1996, scientists working in the Dafeng Milu Nature Reserve found one mother feeding two infants in the artificial breeding herd. After observation, they confirmed that one of the infant deer was born to another mother. In the summer of 2004, it was found for the first time that one mother fed three infant deer at the same time in the artificial breeding herd in the Taihu Xishan Milu Breeding Base in Suzhou. According to the breeding records at that time, the three infants being suckled by the same mother deer were born of three different mothers. This phenomenon shows that a female Père David's deer can act as a "foster mother"with enough milk to spare for all.

• A female breastfeeding three infant deer.

• Infant deerbeing suckled milk.

VI

Père David's Deer
Feeding Habits

Cogon, hornworts, water milfoil, raupo, water chives and other aquatic plants are the favorite foods of the Père David's deer. Every year in late April, when the temperature reaches 12 ℃ , the aquatic plants gradually float to the surface, and the Père David's deer begin to go to water and eat these tender plants. Sometimes when the plants have not grown to the water surface, the Père David's deer cannot wait and plunge their mouths beneath the surface in search of delicacies. They can even keep both eyes open underwater to find food. In order to eat the aquatic plants deep in the water, the Père David's deer often pull up the grass by the roots, bringing many plants floating to the surface.

    Spartina alterniflora is also popular. It is not original to China, but was introduced from abroad in the 1970s. Planted along coastal

• Raupo.

• Inula flower.

• Microstegium nodosum.

• Pennisetum alopecuroides.

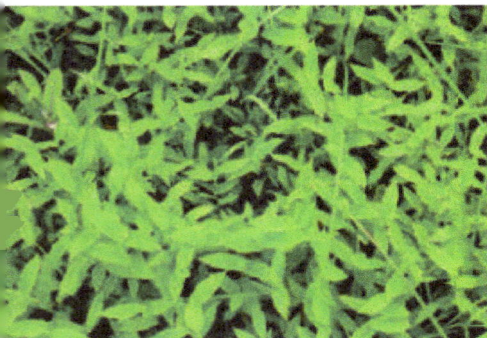

• Oplismenus compositus.

• Cogon.

beaches, it can play the role of retaining tidewater like a protective seawall, and in accumulating mud. As the climate and the environment of China's coastal beaches are very suitable for the growth of Spartina alterniflora, it grows fast and vigorously along the eastern beaches, so that many local species have gradually been reduced.

In the early spring of 2007, scientists in Jiangsu Dafeng Milu Nature Reserve were first to discover that wild Père David's deer could eat Spartina alterniflora. It not only solves the difficulties of food shortage during a period of no concealment in winter and early spring for wild Père David's deer, but also restrains the growth of this invasive alien species.

VII

Individual Behavior of the Père David's Deer

Père David's Deer Can Swim

Swimming is one of the basic survival skills of the Père David's deer. According to local records of Nantong in Jiangsu Province, several hundred years ago, people saw Père David's deer swimming from islands in the sea to the mainland. After eating to fulfillment on land, they carried grass on their heads and swam back to the island. In 1997, when the middle reaches of the Yangtze River suffered a catastrophic flood, more than 60 Père David's deer swam across the Yangtze River from Shishou on the north bank to Huarong on the southern side.

In the water, when an infant deer has no

• Young Père David's Deer crossing waters.

strength to swim, the mother will carry it on her back, guarding the infant to swim ashore.

Père David's deer is a wetland animal, and it cannot be separated from water areas. In the nature reserves of the Père David's deer, it is a common scene that little deer chase each other in the shallows, mother deer walk leisurely in the water, pairs of male deer fight in the water, and groups of deer run through the water creating surging waves around them. Some Père David's deer submerge their bodies in the water, leaving only the head above the surface. This is not

• Swimming across a river.

• Chasing each other in water.

only for bath and cooling purposes, but can also prevent the bites from blood-sucking insects. It is a self-protection behavior of the Père David's deer. Other Père David's deer often take a walk in deep water, and then return to the shore, shaking off the water on their body, as if to relieve fatigue and become full of energy suddenly.

Père David's Deer Can 'Stand up'

The Père David's deer is a large mammal walking on four legs, but sometimes it can"stand up"and walk on its two hind legs. In winter people often see in the living area two males jump at the same time, stand up on their two hind legs, thus fighting each other with their two forelimbs, and move forward or backward together. As if choreographed, one deer moves forward and the other moves backward, just like in social dancing. Sometimes they jump and fight each other for fun on the spot, and sometimes they jump and fight for fun while walking two to five meters away. Males often do this in the season when growing velvet antlers, but have to be especially careful to prevent injuring their new antlers. Female deer, without antlers, can also jump and stand up to fight all year round. Sometimes two Père David's deer raise their two forelimbs and fight each other while standing on their two hind legs at disputes with each other or dissatisfaction with a situation.

• Two jumping female deer.

• Two jumping male deer.

• Traces along a mountain path of plants eaten by Père David's deer.

☐ Père David's deer Can Climb Mountains

Since ancient times, Père David's deer lived on the low-altitude plains and wetlands, becoming a typical wetland animal. However, they can also cross steep slopes and climb mountains.

In 2005, a herd of Père David's deer were in bred artificially at the foot of Dongpo Mountain in Lin'an City, Zhejiang Province. They often sought food in the mountains with a vertical height of nearly 200 meters. When climbing the mountain, they would leap over abrupt rock faces with gradients between 60 and 80 degrees and heights of about 2 meter, or take an oblique-line and sidle upward to slopes with gradients between 40 and 60 degrees. In walking, they would eat the plants growing along the slopes to supplement their nutritional needs.

There are two reasons for the Père David's deer to climb mountains. First, they have to climb and cross the mountain barriers in order to escape the attack of natural enemies, look for new food sources, or migrate due to climate changes. Secondly, caused by artificial factors, the wetlands suitable for the Père David's deer are occupied by human beings, and in the mountains, they have no choice but to learn to climb.

• Herd of Père David's deer at the foot of a mountain.

• Sleeping in a sitting position.

Sleeping Position of Père David's Deer

There are three kinds of sleeping positions adopted by Père David's deer. Firstly, they sleep in a sitting position with two hind legs bent under the belly and two forelimbs in a half-kneeling posture. Second, they sleep in a standing position, with four limbs upright, head, neck and body in a line with the same longitudinal axis, and a drooping tail. Thirdly, they sleep in a lying position with the whole body on the ground and four limbs stretched out straight. The sitting position is the most common, the standing position is relatively rare, and the lying position is extremely rare. The Père David's deer generally go to sleep after having eaten enough and to restore their spirit and strength through sleep.

• Sleeping in a lying position.

• Sleeping in a standing position.

VIII

Associated Animals of
Père David's Deer

The associated animals of the Père David's deer include magpies, egrets, cattle back herons, dragonflies, etc. They live together with the Père David's deer in the meadow wetlands, accompanying each other and becoming inseparable.

• Egrets and young Père David's.

• Magpies and Père David's deer.

IX

Co-existence and Common Development with Humans

From near extinction to returning to their homeland, and then to the regeneration of modern wild populations, the Père David's deer has escaped the sentence of extinction. All these factors are closely related to human activity. Today, in the homeland of Père David's deer–China–the ecological environment is constantly improving, with the basic conditions for species prosperity. At the same time, with the continuous expansion of international exchanges, the Père David's deer can be seen all over the world. People are doing their best to study and protect them. We humans and deer can happily co-exist.

www.ingramcontent.com/pod-product-compliance
Lightning Source LLC
Chambersburg PA
CBHW041217030426
42336CB00023B/3372